First published in Great Britain in 2025 by:

Young Writers
Remus House
Coltsfoot Drive
Peterborough
PE2 9BF
Telephone: 01733 890066
Website: www.youngwriters.co.uk

All Rights Reserved
Book Design by Neila Cepulionyte
© Copyright Contributors 2025
Softback ISBN 978-1-83685-499-9
Printed and bound in the UK by BookPrintingUK
Website: www.bookprintinguk.com
YB0641Q

FOREWORD

Welcome Reader,

For Young Writers' latest competition *Wonderverse*, we asked primary school pupils to explore their creativity and write a poem on any topic that inspired them. They rose to the challenge magnificently with some going even further and writing stories too! The result is this fantastic collection of writing in a variety of styles.

Here at Young Writers our aim is to encourage creativity in children and to inspire a love of the written word, so it's great to get such an amazing response, with some absolutely fantastic pieces. This open theme of this competition allowed them to write freely about something they are interested in, which we know helps to engage kids and get them writing. Within these pages you'll find a variety of topics, from hopes, fears and dreams, to favourite things and worlds of imagination. The result is a collection of brilliant writing that showcases the creativity and writing ability of the next generation.

I'd like to congratulate all the young writers in this anthology, I hope this inspires them to continue with their creative writing.

CONTENTS

Ashley Road Primary School, Aberdeen

Aboelgasim Abdelgadir (8)	1
Heidi Robertson (8)	2
Serena Magodo (8)	3
Rory Swankie (8)	4
Holly Wilson (8)	5
Abhyuday Baswan (9)	6
Adam Abdel Mageed (8)	7
Flora Barras (8)	8
Harrison Cameron (8)	9
William Christie (8)	10
Amber Watson (8)	11
Millie Thomson (8)	12
Amelia Duncan (8)	13
Grace Oyebamiji (8)	14
Brodie Forbes (8)	15
Saiorse Cullen (9)	16
Isabella Fowler (9)	17
Ella Taylor (8)	18
Ramsey Rothwell (8)	19
Yaz Reid (8)	20
Farah Ramazanova (8)	21
Izzy Reid (8)	22
Alex Gray (8)	23
Lucy Meredith (8)	24
Excel Emokhare (8)	25
Sonny Robertson (8)	26
Arthur Atkins (9)	27
David Smaranda (8)	28
Nicole Ikharia (8)	29
Finlay Shaw (8)	30
Eisley Berglund (8)	31
Martha Leslie (8)	32
Zara Ubaid (8)	33
Gaurav Ashokan (9)	34
Beverly Adedokun (8)	35
Oliver Burgess (8)	36
Coby Brown (8)	37
Tommaso Papi (8)	38
Ellis Munro-Burns (9)	39
Gray Lawtie (8)	40
Ella Shaw (8)	41
Kenzi Carneson (8)	42
Arran Duncan (8)	43
Jessica Bell (8)	44
Nataniel (8)	45
Rosie Reid (8)	46
Henry Klen	47
Matthew Sim (9)	48
Mina Maghami (9)	49
Albin Nip (8)	50
George Medlock (8)	51

De Vere Primary School, Castle Hedingham

Autumn Whalley (10) & Rosie Smith	52
Thomas Beck (11) & Edmund	54
Zara Joshua (11)	56
Dylan Peacock (11) & Freddie Totman (11)	57
George Pettit (10)	58
Esmee Coleman (10) & Dinasha	59
Neive Catterwell (10)	60
Bethany Shears (11)	61
Paige Biggs (11) & Layla May Franklin (11)	62

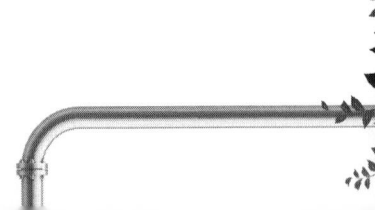

Dulverton Junior School, Dulverton

Darcey Rees (11)	63
Tom Sampson (10)	64
Eve Tolman (10)	66
Elsie Beck (10)	68
Patricia Polinska (10)	69
Florence Smith-Paine (11)	70
Daisy Wickenden (11)	71
Penelope Ingram (11)	72
Lily Yeates (11)	73
Orla Scandrett (10)	74
Toby Routley (11)	75
Thomas Eales (11)	76
Oscar Ratcliffe (10)	77
Harry Passmore (11)	78
Catherine Herbert (11)	79

Elston Hall Primary School, Fordhouses

Zoya Yadgar Ali (8)	80
Timosin James (9)	81
Jivraj Singh Kainth (9)	82
Jaiya Preet Kaur Sidhu (8)	83
Phoebe Shannon (9)	84
Riley Bryan (8)	85
Saffiya Anderson (8)	86
Zara Moustfa (8)	87
Jesse Daka (8)	88
Jaime-Lei Cohen (9)	89
Aadhya Golya (8)	90
Miyah Jackson-Tait (8)	91
Jayden Hyde (8)	92
Isabella Hayward (8)	93
Mikhail Khan (9)	94
Aemilla Hawkes (9)	95
Eliza Hanson (9)	96
Ella Yassin (9)	97
Corbyn Goffe (9)	98
Jack Evans (9)	99
Oliver Jackson (8)	100
Oliver Fletcher (8)	101
Alisha Kaur (8)	102
Matheson Connelly-Beck (8)	103
Mollie Slade (9)	104
Sarah Asampana (9)	105
Arlo Chander (9)	106
Eden Blair (8)	107
George Bridges (8)	108
Emmy Rogers (9)	109
Taran Johal (8)	110
Gurfateh Kharoud (9)	111
Nairi Rogers (8)	112
Heidi Cadman (9)	113
Reuben Solomon (9)	114
Talia Bennett (8)	115
Krihaan Patel (9)	116
Garrett Newey (8)	117
Leah Francis (9)	118
Gurveer Aujla (9)	119
Lilly-Jean Case (9)	120
Aubree Phillips (9)	121
Jessica Roberts (8)	122
Isla Burke (8)	123
Imogen Dearn (8)	124
Joel Kevin (9)	125
Leo Tavaris (8)	126
Cian McGuinness (8)	127
Christian Betts (9)	128
Micheala Kandare (8)	129
Amelia Motsi (8)	130
Jenson Corbett (8)	131
Isabelle Martin (8)	132
James Hayward (8)	133
Alessandro Boneham (8)	134
Kate Wilkinson (9)	135
Presley Keogh (8)	136
Liliana Silba (8)	137
Flynn Ballinger-Heeney (9)	138
Sara Mohammed (9)	139
Ivor Richards (8)	140
Scarlett Page (8)	141
Amelia Van Falier (9)	142
Emma Watkiss (8)	143
Caelan Spittle (8)	144

Billy Guest (8)	145
Owens Osagie (8)	146
Harry Latham (9)	147
Olivia Knott (8)	148
Maseda Bobie (8)	149
Farid Ahmed Ibrahim (9)	150
Peyton Justin (8)	151
Matthew Powis (9)	152
Chijioke Nwoye (9)	153
Olievia Coyne (9)	154
Lilly Sohal (8)	155
Charlie Jones (8)	156
Hugo Jenkins (9)	157
Noah Lea (9)	158
Daisy Durnall (9)	159
Corey Marsden (9)	160
Bradley Wood (8)	161
Reece Archer (8)	162

Gladestry Church-In-Wales Primary School, Gladestry

Arthur Jauncey-Wellard (8)	163
Jerry James (7)	164
Romy Gent (7)	165

St Bartholomew's Primary School, Glasgow

Iyanuoluwa Oni (11)	166
Annie Moffat (11)	167
Frankie McGuire (11)	168
Ioana Mandici (11)	169
Riley Hart (10)	170
Kacey McCallion (11)	171
Stephen Ross (11)	172
Deyvid Mitsanov (10)	173

St Oswald's RC Primary School, Wrekenton

Maria Lejwoda (9)	174
Violet Dixon (9)	175
Elisha Nouaffo (8)	176

Roxy-Judith Murphy (8)	177
Ellie-Mae Cooper (8)	178
Anna Galach (8)	179
James Donnelly (9)	180
Isaac Hand (8)	181
Ella Fairless (9)	182
Max Nalepka (8)	183
Julia Jablonska (9)	184
Bobby Buxton (8)	185
Thomas Reveley	186
Tommy Alberts (8)	187
Jacob Hewitson (8)	188
Kuba Malocha (8)	189
Scarlett Coulson (8)	190

St Stephen's RC Primary School, Blairgowrie

Fia Tennant (11)	191
Amanda Miller (11)	192
Elsie Watt (11)	194
Richard Mcgregor (12)	196
Liam Nelson (11)	198
Karolina Peplinska (11)	199

Swallow Dell Primary School, Welwyn Garden City

Ava Allen-Goring (11)	200
Freya Bartell (11)	202
Jack Horton (10)	203
Ellis Winward (11)	204
Adam Benbassou (11)	206
Jessica Phillips (10)	207
Amira Benbassou (9)	208

The Belsteads School, Little Waltham

Sasha Morton (14)	209
Skyla Kay-Parsons (12)	210
Adam Morris (15)	211
Frankie Witham (13)	212
Anne-Marie Smith (13)	213

Angus Macmillan   214
Bella Oates   215

Thornhill Primary School, Shildon

Byron-William Booth (11)   216
Nell Egglestone (10)   217

Ysgol Parcyrhun, Ammanford

Gayuni Balasuriya (10)   218
Efa Jones (8)   219
Elinor Davies (7)   220

THE POEMS AND STORIES

Adventure In Space

U ranus has some tiny clouds in it, *whoosh, whoosh and whoosh.*

N eptune takes over two hundred years to get to Concord speed.

I ce giants have tiny water in Uranus and Neptune remains in the form of ice.

V enus, clouds of acid cover the surface where the temperature is high enough to melt lead.

E arth, the third 'rock' from the sun is unique in many ways.

R ockets, the flame of an Apollo launch lights the night sky.

S tars birth, a star is a huge ball of hydrogen and gas lit up by nuclear reactions in its core.

E clipses, total eclipses of the sun are a spectacular sight.

Aboelgasim Abdelgadir (8)
Ashley Road Primary School, Aberdeen

Max My Dog

B ack in my family, I had a brother who was cute and cuddly,
A nd his name was Max and his surname was Robertson.
C lever was what my mum called Max when he was clever.
K ind and gentle, he liked always speaking to Max.

T hen when I cuddled him, he would lie down on my lap and snuggle as cuddly as a kitten.
H e always liked to get cuddles from anyone around.
E very day, he sat down in front of his bowl and waited for food to come.
N orth and east my dog liked to walk, as the breeze stretched through his fur.

Heidi Robertson (8)
Ashley Road Primary School, Aberdeen

Moon And Pup Go Together

Moon is sad,
Pup is mad,
But they were both very annoyed,
'Cause both weren't in a clan.

Pup started barking in the middle of space,
She scratched the stars but left no trace,
Moon was so badly crying,
While Pup was still gravity-defying.

Both just floated around helplessly,
It was as scary as being stuck up a tree,
Both of them just wander,
Until they found each other.

So Moon was sad,
Pup was mad,
Until they met each other,
Then started their own clan.

Serena Magodo (8)
Ashley Road Primary School, Aberdeen

Haikus About Food

Scrambled egg
Eggs, you are yummy
Scrambled is my favourite egg
Why are you so good?
Poached egg
Did you come from space?
Why are you so good, poached egg?
Are you in my world?
Boiled egg
The burst of yolk, wow!
When I put toast in, delish
How did you get here?
Fried egg
Your egg white is wow
Fried egg, you are so delish
All eggs are delish
Toast
With jam, you are wow
I love you with every spread
You are amazing.

Rory Swankie (8)
Ashley Road Primary School, Aberdeen

Oh, Spring

Oh, spring,
How tulips look like sweets and in spring you find big brown feet,
Oh, spring,
All the deer coming out of their little cosy homes and smelling the flowers with their little black nose,
Oh, spring,
You really are great, the mini monkeys with leaves on their face and tickling people's hands and feet,
Oh, spring,
You're as sweet as sweeties if there were only winter, autumn and summer,
Oh, spring,
You're my lover!

Holly Wilson (8)
Ashley Road Primary School, Aberdeen

Vietnam War

V ietnamese trying their best by setting landmines.
I t is only for the brave.
E veryone needs to brace.
T anks as big as Jupiter.
N ever mess with the people in the war.
A gainst the resourceful Americans.
M en march in training.

W *ham! Bang! Crash!*
A rtilleries are loading every now and then.
R un! Run! Retreat! *Retreat!*

Abhyuday Baswan (9)
Ashley Road Primary School, Aberdeen

Dragons

D ragons are amazing creatures that can fly as fast as a rocket
R emember, remember that dragons are not for messing about
A lright, alright, *boom!* I am going to save you
G o, go, run away, someone's on their way into the night to save the day
O h dragons, why? Why? Why are you killing people?
N ight comes, *never go out!*
S unlight comes, no dragons are here.

Adam Abdel Mageed (8)
Ashley Road Primary School, Aberdeen

Imagination

I deas as bright as the sun
M agical myths dance across the mind
A s those myths become reality
G reat minds think alike, yet differently
I n this void, bad thoughts go *pop!* Your mind takes over
N o idea is bad
A n amazing world of colour
T ime flies by
I magination is key to success
O riginal ideas
N ever ends.

Flora Barras (8)
Ashley Road Primary School, Aberdeen

About Dinosaurs

D inosaurs stomp like an angry person,
I like dinosaurs because they *roar!*
N o dinosaurs are alive right now,
O mnivores are a type of dinosaur that eats greens,
S ome dinosaurs eat dinosaurs,
A dinosaur is as loud as a volcano,
U nderwater dinosaurs go *splash*,
R eckless, running dinosaurs are fast.

Harrison Cameron (8)
Ashley Road Primary School, Aberdeen

All About Dogs

A mazing dogs
L abradoodle love
L et your dog play.

A ll dogs are cute
B eagles are smart
O h, dogs, you're all so lovely
U p and down the stairs
T reats are yummy.

D ogs are cute
O h, golden doodle
G ood golly
S weet dogs.

William Christie (8)
Ashley Road Primary School, Aberdeen

Winter, Spring, Summer, Autumn

Haiku poetry

Sparkly, slippery
Beautiful, cold, and crunchy
Ice freezes water.

In spring, flowers spring
And Easter is exciting
And bunnies come out.

Summer sun shines bright
In summer you can go to
The beach and have fun!

In autumn, the trees'
Leaves go yellow and orange
Leaves fall off the trees.

Amber Watson (8)
Ashley Road Primary School, Aberdeen

Moon Dog

M agical Moon Dog lives on the moon
O r silly with not much to do
O r it's not normal for a dog to live on the moon
N ot strange that she has stars on her fur

D oesn't want to go to Earth
O r she is a fictional character
G ood she doesn't know that Moon Dog isn't real.

Millie Thomson (8)
Ashley Road Primary School, Aberdeen

The Cuteness Of Rats

Oh, rats,
I love you so much,
That even just one touch,
It feels like too much.
Oh, rats,
How I love when you're on my head,
And how you force me out of bed.
Oh, rats,
I love how with just one creak,
You make a big *squeaaak!*
Oh, rats,
You are the best pet ever,
And nothing could be better.

Amelia Duncan (8)
Ashley Road Primary School, Aberdeen

Amazing

A n astronaut is a person who goes to visit space.
M oving out of space takes a long time.
A mazing planets to see in the wonderful space.
Z ooming through space is fun.
I love space because there are lots of planets.
N o animals are in space, not even birds.
G oing to space is fun.

Grace Oyebamiji (8)
Ashley Road Primary School, Aberdeen

A Penguin

P enguins are super small when born
E xcellent divers for going down deep
N asty fish are what penguins eat
G nawing is what penguins do when eating
U nder the ice the fish are hard to find
I ntelligent penguins are good at diving
N oisy penguins are very annoying.

Brodie Forbes (8)
Ashley Road Primary School, Aberdeen

Save Our Future

F lowers, trees, plants and all
U nderstand that something's wrong
T he planet needs our help. Come on, please
U ngrateful for our amazing planet, we are all
R un all you like, but it would still be our fault
E veryone, just help the planet and also save us all.

Saiorse Cullen (9)
Ashley Road Primary School, Aberdeen

Gross Goblins

G ruesome goblins stumbling about.
O n the cliff lies their home.
B *ang!* The sound of cannons.
L ying around on the rocks.
I n their homes lies a powerful rock.
N othing else to do, sitting boredly about.
S leep all night and awake all day.

Isabella Fowler (9)
Ashley Road Primary School, Aberdeen

An Ode To A Duck

Oh, Duck,
How I love you so.
Your beak is so orange
And you're so nice, Duck.
I love you, Duck.
Oh, Duck,
I just can't tell you
How much I love you.
If I do, you will fall asleep.
Oh, Duck,
You are so fluffy
And your flappy feet
Are so flappy.

Ella Taylor (8)
Ashley Road Primary School, Aberdeen

Evil Carrot Scientist

S cientists are smart, except this one,
C uckoo all the time.
I ntelligent, kind of, at least.
E vil.
N ew experiments.
T all, according to him
I ssues all the time
S uper, according to him
T otal idiot all the time.

Ramsey Rothwell (8)
Ashley Road Primary School, Aberdeen

Friends

F riendly forever
R espect each other
I nclude your friends
E xplore your feelings
N ever hurt each other
D on't shout at anyone.

Friends are important
Friends always care about things
Never start a fight.

Yaz Reid (8)
Ashley Road Primary School, Aberdeen

Bluebird

B eautiful bluebird
L ovely bluebird
U p high in the sky
E ating worms as juicy as an apple
B luebirds are really nice
I ncredible at flying
R eally good at finding juicy worms
D o not like fireworks that pop!

Farah Ramazanova (8)
Ashley Road Primary School, Aberdeen

Glowing Flower

As a flower fell from a blossom tree
I locked the house with a golden key
I turned around, and the flower started to glow
It was something very new to me
It was pink, white and even blue
So I decided to tell my mum and dad
But I thought they would be very mad.

Izzy Reid (8)
Ashley Road Primary School, Aberdeen

My Favourite Food

Pizza
Pizza is crunchy,
Pizza is delicious,
Gooey, good pizza.

Egg on toast
Egg on toast is good,
Egg on toast is so squishy,
Egg on toast is great.

Soup
Soup is watery,
Carrot, tomato, both good,
I like soup with bread.

Alex Gray (8)
Ashley Road Primary School, Aberdeen

Tub-Man

T ub-Man is a great new superhero
U nique superheroes.
B rilliant, bad villains like Frankenstein

M ad, mad supervillain with evil eyes
A sidekick called the King of Ducks
N *ee-naw* as police race with trucks.

Lucy Meredith (8)
Ashley Road Primary School, Aberdeen

Saturn

S aturn is the second-largest planet in our solar system
A stronauts pass in their space crafts *whoosh*!
T oo far to see from Earth.
U ranus is its neighbour.
R ings are made out of Mentos.
N ever go to Saturn.

Excel Emokhare (8)
Ashley Road Primary School, Aberdeen

Ode To King Of Ducks

Oh, King of Ducks,
How I love you,
Your small concussion on your toe is sad,
Your allergy to ice cream is so sad.

You are Tubman's amazing sidekick,
You died but came back to life,
The evil carrot scientists try to kill you with ice cream.

Sonny Robertson (8)
Ashley Road Primary School, Aberdeen

Planets

P luto is like a small rock
L ight is made from the sun
A stronauts go to the moon
N o one has landed on Venus
E arth is a big candy ball
T he plants are in the solar system
S hining sun is so bright.

Arthur Atkins (9)
Ashley Road Primary School, Aberdeen

Space Adventure

S pace is a place to explore
P uffy planets look pretty cool
A nd you might be the first one to explore these planets
C ertain things like asteroids make bang, boom sounds
E ven if you're sad, you can explore things.

David Smaranda (8)
Ashley Road Primary School, Aberdeen

Homeless Kitten

Haiku poetry

A cold, cute kitten,
In the rain, shaking and scared,
So I took it home.

It was shivering,
So I gave her a blanket,
And I kept her safe.

I love her a lot,
When she is cold, I hug her,
To help keep her safe.

Nicole Ikharia (8)
Ashley Road Primary School, Aberdeen

Minecraft

M arvellous Minecraft
I ncredibly fun
N ever ever bad
E xtra exciting
C razy crafting
R un from mobs
A mazing fighting
F ighting the warden
T rade with villagers.

Finlay Shaw (8)
Ashley Road Primary School, Aberdeen

Spring

S pring flowers.
P retty in spring at the park.
R elaxing on the green grass.
I t is like heaven with the blue sky.
N ature is calming on a spring day.
G igantic beautiful trees above my head.

Eisley Berglund (8)
Ashley Road Primary School, Aberdeen

Robot

R obotic parts from head to toe
O h, robot, you will always be my favourite friend
B *leep, blop, beep* makes my heart beat
O h, robot, just you and me
T he things you do change the world.

Martha Leslie (8)
Ashley Road Primary School, Aberdeen

Spring

S un shining as bright as day
P laying outside for hours
R ustling trees are in the gardens
I nsects are buzzing outside
N ew life is here for us
G rowth of animals in the world.

Zara Ubaid (8)
Ashley Road Primary School, Aberdeen

Victorians

Every day is as boring as a book of pencil sharpenings,
Some people do crime all the time,
As they only have enough money to buy a lime,
When it rains, it goes plop,
World wars are death.

Who are they?

Gaurav Ashokan (9)
Ashley Road Primary School, Aberdeen

Caterpillar

Haiku poetry

They love to eat leaves
They are as green as the grass
They are interesting

What caterpillars eat
They have fun on leaves
They munch on the leaves to eat
They taste like the grass.

Beverly Adedokun (8)
Ashley Road Primary School, Aberdeen

Untitled

T ikTok App is fun
I showed videos on TikTok
K SI on the internet.
T ikTok got banned in America
O liver loves TikTok
K aty Perry is on TikTok too.

Oliver Burgess (8)
Ashley Road Primary School, Aberdeen

Family

D elightful Daisy
A ctive and fast
I ntelligent like an elephant
S *plat, splat, splat* goes her food
Y oung Daisy loves to run after us and loves hugs!

Coby Brown (8)
Ashley Road Primary School, Aberdeen

Ocean

O h, the ocean is so lovely
C orals are so beautiful and nice
E ntertaining ocean is fun
A fantastic life in the ocean
N othing is as nice as the ocean.

Tommaso Papi (8)
Ashley Road Primary School, Aberdeen

Vikings

V ictorious, vile, vicious
I mmortal
K ill, kidnap
I mmense, insane
N asty, negative, nosy
G igantic, ghastly
S oul scary.

Ellis Munro-Burns (9)
Ashley Road Primary School, Aberdeen

Dogman!

D angerous for bad guys
O nly helpful hero
G oes places at 1,000 mph
M onday to Sunday work
A s fast as a cheetah
N ormal hero.

Gray Lawtie (8)
Ashley Road Primary School, Aberdeen

Cute

C ute, amazing, great guinea pigs,
U nder the wood shavings, wriggling about!
T he guinea pigs make squeaking sounds
E very guinea pig is so cute.

Ella Shaw (8)
Ashley Road Primary School, Aberdeen

Animals

A haiku

Fox frantically hides
Birds as colourful as day
Splash! Croc is playing.

Kenzi Carneson (8)
Ashley Road Primary School, Aberdeen

Dogman

D ogman saves people
O n a mission
G reat bones to eat
M ysteries to solve
A mazing Dogman
N ever mess with dogs.

Arran Duncan (8)
Ashley Road Primary School, Aberdeen

Cats And Kittens

Once, there was a family of cats
That sat on mats with their hats,
Suddenly, a dog came with rice,
So nice, like paradise,
And now we sit where they sat!

Jessica Bell (8)
Ashley Road Primary School, Aberdeen

Beautiful Space

A haiku

Space is beautiful
If there was no Earth, we'd die
The Milky Way - great.

Nataniel (8)
Ashley Road Primary School, Aberdeen

Space Triplets

S pace is awesome
P lanets are where we live
A liens are green
C razy aliens are not nice
E arth is where we live!

Rosie Reid (8)
Ashley Road Primary School, Aberdeen

Bob The Robot

A haiku

The tiny robot
Bob the Robot was his name
He is cute and kind.

Henry Klen
Ashley Road Primary School, Aberdeen

Sugar And Candy

Sweets falling down,
From the sugary cotton candy clouds,
Sugar should be fine,
Because it is truly divine.

Matthew Sim (9)
Ashley Road Primary School, Aberdeen

Dig, Dog

D og quickly digs deep
O ut of view he feels cool
G oing to fetch a very big bouncy ball.

Mina Maghami (9)
Ashley Road Primary School, Aberdeen

Space

A haiku

The sun is a star
Planets are candy in space
Dwarf planets are small.

Albin Nip (8)
Ashley Road Primary School, Aberdeen

Penguins

A haiku

They are tall and cold
Baby ones are very cute
Penguins make huddles.

George Medlock (8)
Ashley Road Primary School, Aberdeen

Renewable Energy

The sun shines like gold,
Golden rivers of sunshine
Sparkling on the world.

Whisper secrets to the Earth,
Solar panels catching the light.

Endlessly blowing,
Twirling across the grey sky,
Dancing around the turbines.

Wind turbines harming all birds,
Out at sea or taking land.

Warmly rising up,
Steam erupting from the Earth
Like a secret fire.

Mysteriously glowing,
Silently dripping to the ground.

Splashing rapidly,
Flowing down the waterfall,
Endlessly surging.

Singing songs of strength and power,
Lively, going down the stream.

Vibrantly growing,
The plants stretch towards the sun,
Naturally forming.

Like nature's gift, shining bright,
Silently burning away.

Peacefully protect
The future that smiles with hope,
Preserving the world.

Make the world a better place
By stopping the fossil fuels.

Autumn Whalley (10) & Rosie Smith
De Vere Primary School, Castle Hedingham

Sustainability

Warmth into the ground,
Deep into the land rise up
A fire below.

The power plants harness heat,
Catching energy under.

A breeze in the sky,
Is caught by a lone structure,
Spinning in the air.

The wind turbine makes power,
But is a killer of birds.

The sun brightly shines,
Its beams reflect down below
Endless energy.

The expenses skyrocket high,
As it is too expensive.

The golden water,
Flows through a large damn quickly,
Spinning the turbines.

Cool, blue, infinite power,
Will never, ever run out.

The plants are burnt away,
Life grows to use for power,
Renewable heat.

You silly people,
Burning many bad fuel types,
It's very naughty.

Use lots of clean energy,
Or you'll kill our planet.

Thomas Beck (11) & Edmund
De Vere Primary School, Castle Hedingham

Look Up At The Stars

I lay my eyes on the whimsical sky
The shimmers from the moon gazed upon me
It was like a dream
In fact, it was a dream so real.

Swoosh!
The breeze swept past me in an instant
The elegant beauty of the stars blinded upon me.

Buzz!
The shooting star dashed through the sky
It was like a burst of excitement
That feeling I was feeling was astonishment
Something I had never felt before
Something new
Or something so amazing I would want to squeal.

For me, the sky and the stars are something worth looking at.

Zara Joshua (11)
De Vere Primary School, Castle Hedingham

The Energy Earth

Glowing like the sun
As bright as a thousand tiny stars
The sun heats the Earth
Electricity is key
Solar power helps the world.

The wind, calm and smooth
Turbines are very helpful
Wind power is good
Spinning around whenever
Wind energy helps the Earth.

It uses water
It can destroy habitats
Lots of energy
High risk to civilisation
It is very dangerous.

Made from plants and leaves
It can burn, so that's bad
It comes from trees
Animal waste is smelly
Don't hurt animals, okay?

Dylan Peacock (11) & Freddie Totman (11)
De Vere Primary School, Castle Hedingham

World War II

From that very moment,
I was told to leave,
Everything changed.

I had to holster a gun,
Every country I roamed.
I was no longer allowed to see my family.
Knowing that one shot of a gun could kill a man,
I was as cautious as ever.

As the days went on,
The battle raged on.
Soon, I lost contact with my family.
I would write and write yet no answer.

Would I ever see my family again?
Would I survive this battle?

God knows.

George Pettit (10)
De Vere Primary School, Castle Hedingham

Renga Poem

The world is dying
Stop causing pollution now
Don't use fossil fuels
The world is falling apart
We need to take to live

Hydroelectric
The cold water flows
Rapidly splashing downhill
Waterfalls sing songs
Flowing like a river's heart
The river hums as it turns

The wind
The wind swiftly moves
It is quiet, like a mouse
Blows all around
Swirling, dances in the sky
Pushing blades for energy
Goodbye.

Esmee Coleman (10) & Dinasha
De Vere Primary School, Castle Hedingham

Renewable Energy

Cool, blue, splashing waves,
Flowing, splashing water,
Endless energy.

Cool, splashing waves are very
Flowing the big, blue waves.

Deep under the ground,
Hidden away underneath,
Gives us energy.

Powerful, endlessly breezy,
The endless blowing breeze.

Clean fast energy,
Golden light comes from the sun,
Peaceful energy.

Warm and golden gives us light,
The sparkling sun gives us energy.

Neive Catterwell (10)
De Vere Primary School, Castle Hedingham

The Rules Of Friendship Rights

F ight for your rights
R espect your boundaries
I nclude you in everything
E ncourage you
N ever disrespect you
D efend you
S tand up for you at all costs.

Bethany Shears (11)
De Vere Primary School, Castle Hedingham

Electricity

The sun is beaming.
On the beach it's shining.
Endless energy, solar panels
Collect light, giving electricity.

Paige Biggs (11) & Layla May Franklin (11)
De Vere Primary School, Castle Hedingham

Kelpie

Darkness overlapping the ocean.
The sea moving in a sickly motion.
Vines crept and crawled, gripped and grasped the creature's leg.
The wind crippling the earth's interior.
Red roses slowly turning to black.
The hooves pounding the sand, hoofprints following flat.
Ghastly words, hardly stopping for a chat.
The beast rose from the sea, its obsidian eyes gleaming.
The deep waves whispering, hollow dreams scheming.
The long flowy mane, leaking through the water.
Kelpie emerged from the loch.
The sweaty limb, vines up his hoch.
Spirits reaching their final destinations.
Why this place? Of all locations?
Darkness folding its crippled back, lost in mutations.
He was rotten, you see... Kelpie let out a whinny.
Bony and skinny.
The branches on his head, reaching for the dark sky.
He galloped the sand, letting out a low cry.
Dark skies came rolling in.
Deep green moss, clinging on his shin.

Darcey Rees (11)
Dulverton Junior School, Dulverton

Whispering Death

A street lamp flickers,
An owl bickers.
The clock strikes three,
He jumps from a tree.
His whispering breath calling for death,
I thought I saw him run his breath,
For I saw his majesty. Whispering death.

I saw the fire spread like dread,
I also saw his crippled head.
Long wispy horns spring from his skin,
The haunting of terror finally begins.
He takes me by the hand and promises relief,
Little does he know I had no belief.
The sky turns black,
I have to go back.
His small burning eyes, burning with fury,
I must go find my dear old Yury.
He glares deep into my eyes,
By the end of the night, one of us dies.
My breath goes cold,
Terror unfolds.
I thought I saw him run his breath,
For I saw him, his majesty. Whispering death.

My hair gets pulled. He pulls me under.
Lightning and thunder lighting the sky,
My face is numb, too numb to cry.
The night draws on,
I call for John.
My voice echoes through the crippled sky,
I question tonight, my heart thinks I'll die.
My cold, crisp skin is no longer dry.
And the world still spins on as all should be,
Even if I'm not there, not even me.
I thought I saw him run his breath,
For I saw him, his majesty. Whispering death.

Tom Sampson (10)
Dulverton Junior School, Dulverton

The Winter Shock?

A twig snapped
The breeze blew
The trees swayed
The night was delayed from eight steps
The eight steps of four girls
Approaching the violence connected the girls
The shock of the girls hit
A small beady eye grew wider
The shortest distance of firing flames shot up
A smell of fish bloomed as three louder footsteps approached

Beautiful bluebells faded as sharp breeze blew
Broken black roses stood dying
Frosty, gloomy figures moved
Blazing blisters buried in their skin
One girl's sight turned
Last memories past
Moments of depression
Breath drained away from her
Bleeding screams grew
The body was pulled
Dying cries bellowed
A thunderbolt of the girls grew

One by one
Each girl heard a voice
A threat of horror
The body appeared
The body was covered with black
Black vessels
The snow turned black as two of the girls remained.

Eve Tolman (10)
Dulverton Junior School, Dulverton

Dachshund Speed

D achshunds are fast
A nimals are friendly
C ute little faces scurrying around
H ounds are cute but a little feisty
S weet faces in the morning
H ounds are cute but a little feisty
U nder the ground, scurrying about
N othing can stop them, nothing in their way
D on't be dismayed, never give up.

S mall, tiny feet pottering around
P *itter, patter, pitter, patter,* the dachshund flashes
E verywhere you go, sausage dogs are around
E ndless surprise, sausage dog surprise
D ogs are nice but sausage dogs are better.

Elsie Beck (10)
Dulverton Junior School, Dulverton

Isadora Makes A Friend

Isadora made a friend,
It was a Glow Sprite,
She had to keep it as a secret,
Nova had forgotten where she had left her toy,
Which is why her burning tears dripped down her face,
They drifted up in the cold and breezy air,
Rushing through the trees like a tornado,
"Oh, lovely, love it,
Finally, I found you,"
Kiss, kiss, kiss,
"Never let you go again,"
Nova soared her toy up in the air,
Feeling as if throwing a beach ball up and down,
Bing. Bong. Beautifully he flew
Posing like a model,
In the pretty chilled air.

Patricia Polinska (10)
Dulverton Junior School, Dulverton

When A Mother Doesn't Love

When I had my first child
Some reason, I couldn't smile
They thought I was crazy
Or maybe I was just lazy

When I returned home
I was utterly alone
And I let out a deep groan

As time went on
The baby grew unbearable
I felt utterly terrible

I suffered nights of insomnia
I couldn't care for her
No matter what I tried
She just cried

When childcare came
I felt deep in shame
Even so, I couldn't help
But smile as she left

After that, I felt free
Like a bird who'd left its tree.

Florence Smith-Paine (11)
Dulverton Junior School, Dulverton

Dreams And Nightmares

You could hear the wind dancing between magenta manes
Hoofbeats thundering down the beach
The sand flying up with the breeze
It was nightfall, and the shimmering water reflected the bright stars
All was silent and still, the perfect night

You could hear the wind snaking between the thorny vines
The dark creatures hunting
It was night, and that's when they came for her
Jaws snarling, and dribble flying
They found her
Then they chased
It galloped as fast as a cheetah
She jumped and fell
Then they pounced with the horn for the prize.

Daisy Wickenden (11)
Dulverton Junior School, Dulverton

Climbing Higher And Higher Every Day

There was a girl born in summer
And she only had brothers,
She liked the everlasting blue and grainy yellow
Down below
And the green up high
Where she could not reach,
She liked climbing up the little branches
Like her brother,
But she couldn't always retreat.

One day, she didn't need help
And she could climb all the way up
And back down without a frown,
When she got to the top,
She was surrounded by the endless greenery
With spots of colour
And at last
She felt free, like a monkey sitting in a tree!

Penelope Ingram (11)
Dulverton Junior School, Dulverton

A Father's Daughter

The clock strikes three,
Could be some type of key,
Every dad's worry,
Every little girl's hurry,
Water stream or a scream,
Dead or alive, a little girl's life,
Drowning or not, you're still counting the lot,
Eyes closing, could try to say your final goodbyes.

One body down, a soul to go,
Making a hole, it's a bit of a stroll,
Swear it's different now that she's gone,
She disappeared, all in one.
Father's daughter,
She's a bit of a walker.

Lily Yeates (11)
Dulverton Junior School, Dulverton

Super Spaniel

S uni saves the day,
U p in the air he flies,
P eople love him,
E nergy never dies,
R elentless surprise.

S uperdog saves the day,
P uppy power, make way,
A happy dog is a happy life,
N ot having a spaniel is not nice,
I f you're in trouble, Super Suni will come straight away,
E ven if you live far away,
L eft and right he flies, then zooms off to go save more lives.

Orla Scandrett (10)
Dulverton Junior School, Dulverton

Winter's Poem

W ilder, the wind whips the evergreen trees.
I n the homes, they celebrate a joyful season.
N ow comes the snow of winter. It's a wonderful time of the year.
T hrough the gusts of the icy wind comes a magical sleigh. Rudolph is here.
E verlasting cheer and smiles continue throughout this glorious time of the year.
R ealising that Saint Nick is always checking the sleigh of cheer... After all, Christmas is here.

Toby Routley (11)
Dulverton Junior School, Dulverton

The Wonder Of Exmoor

E verything is smelling wonderful, we're up on Exmoor
X -ray vision helps to see the animals
M oorland stretches for miles, a special place in the British Isles
O ak trees holding bees, protecting our future,
O ars stroking water on Wimbleball Lake, *splash, splash, splash,*
R unners racing up and down all around the glory of Exmoor.

Thomas Eales (11)
Dulverton Junior School, Dulverton

The Wonder Of

S kill is key when it comes to science
C hemicals are essential.
I f you fail, you learn a lot.
E ndless fun for everyone.
N ature becoming a scientist's friend.
C ompeting for more data.
E ducation is what you need.

Oscar Ratcliffe (10)
Dulverton Junior School, Dulverton

Wonder Of The Darkness

S tars shining so brightly.
P lanets float around us.
A lien mysteries are still drawing on. Are they real, are they not?
C an I see Neil Armstrong bouncing around?
E veryone lives on Earth. Can we ever really explore space?

Harry Passmore (11)
Dulverton Junior School, Dulverton

The World

T he world is a good place,
H elping nature,
E arth is life.

W ondering stuff,
O pportunities to choose,
R egretting things,
L ife depends on me,
D eath or freedom, who will know?

Catherine Herbert (11)
Dulverton Junior School, Dulverton

The Thunder Dragon

T hrough twilight skies, with wings spread wide
H ailing the thunder that shatters the night.
E lectric and fierce, both ancient and bold

T ail like a whip, sharp and bright
H owling in fury, the dragon's name.
U nveiling its power in flashes of light
N ight splits as the Thunder Dragon flies, nimble and fierce beneath storm-filled skies.
D read fills the air with each mighty roar,
E ndlessly soaring, through wind and through rain.
R uthless and wild, none dare to compare.

D ragons get their claws out to fight and defend themselves!
R oars super loudly and makes loud rumbling sounds.
A Thunder Dragon can make the weather turn into thunder!
G angs up and fights dangerous predators.
O n a rock with apricot and rose scales all over its body.
N ear a moonlit pool, and sleeps with a loud rumble.

Zoya Yadgar Ali (8)
Elston Hall Primary School, Fordhouses

Gorgons Are Always Cool

G ood
O ver the cool factor
R ight all the time
G et excited quickly
O verpowered, broken powers
N ever buzz kills
S uper all the time

A lways super
R ed eyes
E ver so cool

A nd turn people into stone
L osers they are... not
W hen the time comes they party
A lso smart
Y ou should never look into their eyes
S uper

C ool
O n brain IQ 500
O n the brink of too many
L ike to run around.

Timosin James (9)
Elston Hall Primary School, Fordhouses

Time Breather

The Time Breather is whistling
Through the midnight sky
With his wings spread out wide
He can easily burst through
The midnight sky

He can fly and fly
He can fly for ages
But when he is hungry
He hunts with his giant, sharp claws

Don't get too close to the Time Breather
You don't want to fight with him
He will give you a time beam
Or give you a powerful time ball blast

His age is older than time
He can fight a dragon or any other creature
He can use his time power from
The present, the past and the future.

Jivraj Singh Kainth (9)
Elston Hall Primary School, Fordhouses

Unicorn Pegasus

U nique and beautiful
N ever stops
I t makes ashes out of its horn
C an breathe fire like ashes
O ne touch and *boom*! Gone
R ed, orange and yellow colours, like fire
N othing can ever touch it

P retty sparkles, like crystal diamonds
E lectric sparks, like ashes of fire
G o, unicorn, go and be free
A s soon as you touch it it fades away.
S parks like fireworks
U sually fearless
S himmering fur, like the sun is sparkling on you.

Jaiya Preet Kaur Sidhu (8)
Elston Hall Primary School, Fordhouses

Paralyzing Dragon

P urple glowing eyes,
A ll over the earth,
R oaring everywhere,
A re you sure you want to see one?
L asers out of its eyes,
Y es, it'll eat you whole,
Z igzag-shaped teeth,
I wish you'd be gone,
N ever go near one,
G oing to live in a cloud.

D on't worry, they won't find you,
R are dragons,
A re you hungry?
G one to the clouds,
O ne Earth, five paralyzing dragons,
N ever win against them.

Phoebe Shannon (9)
Elston Hall Primary School, Fordhouses

Thunder Dragon

T he dragon eats gold lightning
H ides in the clouds
U nder the sky, they fight predators
N ighttime, they fight and fight
D inner time, they eat their prey
E very day, they go out and get prey
R ed dragons fight with blue dragons

D rink the blue rain
R aining at night, they go out and fight
A ngry dragons eat and eat
G et into the clouds and sleep
O range and red fire comes out of their mouth
N ame their clouds and sleep to get energy.

Riley Bryan (8)
Elston Hall Primary School, Fordhouses

My Unicorn

My unicorn has magical wings
Fly, fly, stretch up to the sky
My unicorn has laser eyes
Pow, pow, it's your time to learn to shoot
My unicorn has a giant, fiery tail
Shake, shake, cover the land in a fiery state
My unicorn has a thorny mane
Rumble, rumble, shake, shake
Move your body and make a spiky mess
My unicorn has a body like a horse
Neigh, neigh, gallop, gallop, clop, clop, shake, shake
My unicorn lives in a thorny forest
Chop, chop, this time your home is in a right state.

Saffiya Anderson (8)
Elston Hall Primary School, Fordhouses

My Beast

My beast has eyes as gold as the sun, it loves to play and have fun,
My beast breathes out fire as bright as a light, and hides away at midnight.
My beast has three enormous heads, but sadly zero beds.
My beast has glistening fur, stroke it gently, hear it purr,
My beast likes to drink rain, look out and you might see it by a drain,
My beast has a long, sparkly tail which swishes much faster than a snail,
My beast has a shiny horn which amazingly can change its form
My beast is a beast that I will love forevermore.

Zara Moustfa (8)
Elston Hall Primary School, Fordhouses

Midnight Dragon

M ust be out at midnight
I ts power best in strength.
D ragon with purple colour.
N ight is perfect for them.
I t can live up to 300 years.
G ood and nice to humans.
H abitat is under rocks.
T ough and not easy to tame.

D ying and getting poached.
R oughly comes in the morning.
A hard dragon to find.
G etting killed.
O ver 100 midnight dragons left in the world.
N ever gets scared.

Jesse Daka (8)
Elston Hall Primary School, Fordhouses

Syren!

Syren, Syren
As scary as a shark
Where did you come from, out of the water?
Syren, Syren is ready to strike
Syren, Syren is ready to prey.

Syren, Syren
A tap on the floor
Waiting for the rain to stop pouring
Syren, Syren, like a watery serpent
Syren, Syren, with poisoned blood.

Syren, Syren
Waiting and waiting
Syren, Syren wagging its tail
Syren, Syren, go to sleep
Rest and rest until you fall asleep
Syren, Syren, have a good night's sleep.

Jaime-Lei Cohen (9)
Elston Hall Primary School, Fordhouses

The Free Animal

The acid breather sneaks up on its prey, rips it apart and gobbles and slurps it up. It breathes acid and has a death stare which shoots out lasers. The acid breather gallops in its enchanted area and likes to take a stop near the lake to drink turquoise/lavender water. The magnificent creature with lavender/turquoise hair leaps over and beyond.
As this creature circles, the sparkle in its hair flies behind, and their mind will be filled with happiness. Their white mane will stand, and their lavender hair will fly.

Aadhya Golya (8)
Elston Hall Primary School, Fordhouses

The Hide-Behind

Feet stomp, *bang, bang, bang,*
As their teeth are as sharp as fangs,
Bigger than skyscrapers,
And claws that can easily rip through
Thousands of papers,
They breathe amber fire,
With horns as sharp as barbed wire,
They are as scaly as lizards,
And are trained by wizards,
As their wings cut through the sky,
Their babies are back at their nest giving out a cry,
Most mysteriously, they have three heads,
And will viciously have a meal that it gets.

Miyah Jackson-Tait (8)
Elston Hall Primary School, Fordhouses

The Four-Headed Dragon

D ark at night, the four-headed dragon flew out of the dark cave
R umbling around the dark, stormy, smoky river
A ll of the dragons came together, looking for a safe place to stay
G ood dragons are being hunted by bad dragons
O n this side of the Four-Headed Dragon River, all must become one
N aughty dragons became nice dragons, which made the river a happy place to stay
S lippery slime party was had at the Four-Headed Dragon River Inn.

Jayden Hyde (8)
Elston Hall Primary School, Fordhouses

Night Whisker

N owhere to be seen as they are always mean,
I dentical to tigers as they both always scream.
G azing at the moon.
H ugging children when it's noon.
T ogether when they cry.

W hilst staring at the sky.
H umming sounds are made,
I n beds where eggs are laid.
S cales are wet and slimy,
K illing things that are tiny.
E ating lost kitties,
R oaring through the cities.

Isabella Hayward (8)
Elston Hall Primary School, Fordhouses

The Beast

The beast's menacing eyes flash like rolling thunder,
The beast slithers through the night sky,
The beast soars high, high, high,
Whipping its tail across the soft clouds,
The beast's tummy rumbles with flames,
And all of a sudden...
Bang! A blaze of fire flies out of its mouth,
The beast then shapes its jaws with knives,
And shoots down,
Onto the ground,
With no energy left for flight,
And no energy left for power and might.

Mikhail Khan (9)
Elston Hall Primary School, Fordhouses

Siren, Siren, Over There

Siren, siren, over there
With that beautiful voice you dare
Siren, siren, over there
Attracting sailors with that voice you dare
Siren, siren, over there
Singing your song, thinking your dinner isn't too long
Siren, siren, over there
With your long black hair you dare
Siren, siren, over there
Looking beautiful on a rock you dare
Siren, siren, over there
Living in rough seas
Siren, siren, over there
That is the end of your day.

Aemilla Hawkes (9)
Elston Hall Primary School, Fordhouses

The Snake Dragon

S ilent shadow, scales so bright,
N ever mess with a dragon,
A ll in flames, it spreads its wings,
K ind and bold, it rules as a king,
E verywhere, its magic glows in the dark,

D eep in caves so dark and cold,
R azor-sharp teeth,
A ll dragons eat meat.
G liding far across the skies.
O ver mountains wild and free,
N othing stops a dragon.

Eliza Hanson (9)
Elston Hall Primary School, Fordhouses

It's A Dragon

It's a dragon, we gotta run!
It's a dragon; get your stuff!
It's coming this way, we gotta hide!
I see fire, it's probably his breath!
We're almost there, just a turn!

Choose a spot!
It doesn't matter which!
Quickly, quickly!
Or you might be...

Dead meat!

Night approaches,
We're safe and sound,
What will happen tomorrow?
I guess... it's bad!

Ella Yassin (9)
Elston Hall Primary School, Fordhouses

My Dragon

M agical, evil dragon that looks gorgeous
Y ou should be scared of this evil, terrifying dragon

D angerous beast ready to strike
R apid-quick feature: teeth are knives. Actually sharpened.
A nd a creature that you can't outrun
G uards are even scared of my dragon!
O nly my dragon does not fight their family.
N ame of my dragon is Hazard Dragon.

Corbyn Goffe (9)
Elston Hall Primary School, Fordhouses

Frost Mander

F orever will be in my heart
R eally sharp claws
O n top of rocks when asserting dominance
S ticky feet
T imely attacks

M ales are longer than females
A ll are poisonous
N ot dangerous unless something causes a threat
D anger to anyone or anything that comes running at them
E yes like ice
R oar is a little squeak.

Jack Evans (9)
Elston Hall Primary School, Fordhouses

Hocky Meldon

H elps men.
O bliterates sharks.
C an hear more Meldons.
K ills their type.
Y ep, in the water.

M ost of them don't have hocky.
E ats big fish and can jump high from the water.
L ikes to eat eagles.
D oesn't eat baby fish.
O f them all, the adults are the best.
N one of them eat baby sharks.

Oliver Jackson (8)
Elston Hall Primary School, Fordhouses

The Spiny Dinosaurs

D inosaurs have spines like knives
I n the dense forests they live
N one have been hunted by other animals
O range is the absolute rarest colour for one
S pines as pointy as bobcats' teeth
A s scary as a bloodthirsty zombie
U seful for destroying things
R eally dangerous to mankind
S pines as big as us human beings.

Oliver Fletcher (8)
Elston Hall Primary School, Fordhouses

Rainbow Beast

R un and jump as fast as you can
A nd it is very scary
I n and out it goes
N o need to run, only when it shouts
B e kind to the beast
O h no, it's coming
W hatever you need it will come to life

B e aware, it
E ats humans
A t caves
S cars on its back
T ests on dragons.

Alisha Kaur (8)
Elston Hall Primary School, Fordhouses

The Crimson Cracken

Bow down to the most powerful beast
The Crimson Cracken lives in caves and
Looms around, it is so beautiful
But really it can turn pigs
Into bacon, it's
As big
As
An iceberg
Be petrified.
The dragon may be able
To fry you, but the
Crimson Cracken can turn you into crimson
If it touches you, *boom!* You are gone
Into oblivion.

Matheson Connelly-Beck (8)
Elston Hall Primary School, Fordhouses

Fire Dragon

F ire-like eyes
I ncredible wings
R oaring loud
E legant wings flying in the sky

D eadly teeth that can chop you in a millisecond
R umbling breath
A mbitious claws curl
G inormous, sharp, threatening claws
O rbiting claws curl on the rock
N eon-red fire comes out its gigantic, smelly mouth.

Mollie Slade (9)
Elston Hall Primary School, Fordhouses

The Acid Dragon

A s it secretly emerges
C autiously, its talons are endlessly sharp
I t spits acid out of its mouth
D ormant

D ragon
R eally invincible
A s big as a house
G ives out good luck, good health, and good strength
O ut of all the dragons, it is a powerful beast
N ever go near a powerful dragon.

Sarah Asampana (9)
Elston Hall Primary School, Fordhouses

The Kitsune

K ills small, little mammals like voles and polecats
I t makes a barrier of crystals from its mouth
T heir enchanted body makes the Kitsune invisible
S urprisingly, they have azure crystals on their back
U sually, they live in Poland and the Arctic
N ever stops running away from mankind
E yes like fiery flames.

Arlo Chander (9)
Elston Hall Primary School, Fordhouses

Lift High, Dragon, Fly!

Fly, dragon, fly in the air of mist
Go, dragon, go as fast as you can
Come straight back if you can
Run, dragon, run until you're done
Sleep, dragon, sleep until you repeat
Lift, dragon, lifting the air of the mist
Lonely dragon, lonely until you find your homie
Leap, dragon, leap up to your feet
Calm, dragon, calm until morning waits.

Eden Blair (8)
Elston Hall Primary School, Fordhouses

The Irish Dragon

The Irish dragon is thin and lean,
The Irish dragon has heads of seventeen,

The Irish dragon has nostrils of holes,
The Irish dragon feasts on moles,

The Irish dragon has the wings of an eagle,
The Irish dragon has a tail of a beagle,

The Irish dragon sometimes gets lonely,
The Irish dragon wants a friend only.

George Bridges (8)
Elston Hall Primary School, Fordhouses

My Baby Flicarrita

My baby Flicarrita
He is really cute. You just gotta know him
My baby Flicarrita
Can't fly yet
My baby Flicarrita
Okay, okay, yes. He falls on his head.

Head of a fox
Body of a lion
Wings of an eagle
Tail of a wolf
Beautiful orchid
Maybe a little blue.

I hope you like my baby Flicarrita!

Emmy Rogers (9)
Elston Hall Primary School, Fordhouses

My Dragon

My dragon has long, spiky scales on his back.
My dragon is almost extinct.
My dragon is as big as a mountain.
My dragon is never to be seen in this world.
My dragon can spit poison right at you.
My dragon is treated very poorly.
My dragon can eat a tree in one bite.
My dragon is elemental.
My dragon likes enchanted forests.

Taran Johal (8)
Elston Hall Primary School, Fordhouses

It Is A Dragon

It has hair.
It has fluffy hair.
It has long legs, like a spider.
Very big stomach, like a whale.
It eats rotten flesh.
It feels weird.
They are not faster than me at all.
They are slow, like a snail.
It is big, like a dragon, like everyone's legends.
It is fluffy, like a bunny.
It is in water, like a fish.

Gurfateh Kharoud (9)
Elston Hall Primary School, Fordhouses

My Dragon

My dragon can fly high above in the sky,
My dragon can shoot a blaze of flames,
My dragon has scarlet red scales,
My dragon has shiny claws and likes to play games.

My dragon is funny and fun,
My dragon's character shines like the sun,
My dragon's kindness knows no end,
My dragon is my bestest friend.

Nairi Rogers (8)
Elston Hall Primary School, Fordhouses

Sea Unicorn

S moothly glides in moonlit pools
E ats the burning embers of a dying fire
A ngrily fights

U nder bushes, she quietly curls up
N oisy
I ntelligent sea unicorn
C urious creature
O rchid tail curls around her
R eally fluffy
N ever happy.

Heidi Cadman (9)
Elston Hall Primary School, Fordhouses

Slender Dragon

D ark purple body with beautiful shining eyes
R aging through the midnight sky
A geing year by year, always getting old
G rabbing food one by one, *munch, munch, munch*
O ver hills, under bushes, where you can find them
N ever hunted, loved by everyone, save my dragon, everyone.

Reuben Solomon (9)
Elston Hall Primary School, Fordhouses

Go, Unicorn, Go!

Fly, unicorn, fly,
High, high, high.

Run, unicorn, run,
Fast, fast, fast.

Drink, unicorn, drink,
Slurp, slurp, slurp.

Eat, unicorn, eat,
Crunch, crunch, crunch.

Gallop, unicorn, gallop,
Quick, quick, quick.

Breathe, unicorn, breathe,
Ahh.

Talia Bennett (8)
Elston Hall Primary School, Fordhouses

My Dragon

My dragon is small but deadly
And cute just to trick you
And as deathly as the Amazon river
Filled with deadly crocodiles
Sleeping in a cave
Eating dirt and seawater
A tail with shimmering gold
And a beautiful diamond colour
They like dipping it in water
And they have a penguin-like body.

Krihaan Patel (9)
Elston Hall Primary School, Fordhouses

Eldertubies

E ldertubies
L ike
D ipsy taking
E very dip in the water
R iver, ocean or lake
T inky-Winky likes going
U nder the tree, meeting
B rave guests
I n the forest there are
E ldertubies, four of them
S uper good friends.

Garrett Newey (8)
Elston Hall Primary School, Fordhouses

Run, Unicorn, Run, Run!

Run, unicorn, run, run!
From mankind

Tiptoe, tiptoe down the hill!

You'll once be safe
Even if your legs are small
You'll once be safe

Run, run, run to your family!

You're safe at home
With your cuddly family
Food is there, and things are fair.

Leah Francis (9)
Elston Hall Primary School, Fordhouses

The Voyster

The Voyster has red legs
He eats meat
His tooth is sharp
Claws
He's cursed, was a dragon
He didn't like other dragons making fun of him
He didn't like other dogs making fun of them
He started being nice to everyone.
He likes to play with everyone.
He likes to make friends.

Gurveer Aujla (9)
Elston Hall Primary School, Fordhouses

Snow Dragon

S nowy
N oble
O pen-minded
W arm fire blows out of his mouth

D eadly like teeth
R oars like thunder
A mbitious dragon to reach higher than before
G inormous sharp claws
O ngoing changes
N oises terrifying people.

Lilly-Jean Case (9)
Elston Hall Primary School, Fordhouses

My Dragon

M y dangerous dragon,
Y ay, yay, yay, I see my dragon.

D angerous with green emerald eyes
R ed, fiery body
A way down south with a sharp, spiky back
G reat dragon
O n the way to find a dragon in a forest
N ever go to my dragon.

Aubree Phillips (9)
Elston Hall Primary School, Fordhouses

Dragon

D o you ever wonder what a real dragon looks like?
R uby red eyes glowing fluorescently
A long, stretchy tail smashing fiercely
G reat sharp teeth biting ferociously
O range glowing scales that shimmer bright
N ow you know what a real dragon looks like.

Jessica Roberts (8)
Elston Hall Primary School, Fordhouses

Lazer Snake

L asers shoot out of eyes
A s small as a cat
Z zzs all day
E ats fish, insects, and grass
R azor-sharp teeth.

S cales as slimy as a snail
N ew forests
A te a human
K ind to owners
E arthy green colour.

Isla Burke (8)
Elston Hall Primary School, Fordhouses

Salmanda

S its on enchanted rocks
A pples are his favourite food
L icks you if you bother him
M an, it's tall, sucks up its food
A nd ends its prey easily
N eon-purple body
D igs for worms
A nd will eat humans if you anger him.

Imogen Dearn (8)
Elston Hall Primary School, Fordhouses

The Frog Dragon

F ire-breathing creature
R eliable with stuff
O ffensive, smart creature
G reen skin

D ragon
R aging sometimes
A nice but strong creature
G reen fire
O n the go all the time
N ice creature.

Joel Kevin (9)
Elston Hall Primary School, Fordhouses

The Beast In The Zoo

Today I'm going to the zoo
I'm going to spot the new beast
Yay, I'm at the zoo
I spotted the new beast
The zookeeper there is gonna be a monster
Enclosure, oh no, it broke out
We need to hide
I rush away
It breathes fire
It has sharp talons.

Leo Tavaris (8)
Elston Hall Primary School, Fordhouses

Cian's Poem

A dragon has claws,
They have fire.
A dragon has wings.

He has fire eyes,
He has golden teeth,
He eats rotten flesh.

My dragon is the rainbow dragon.
The dragon comes out at night to fly around.

In the morning, the dragon goes to sleep.

Cian McGuinness (8)
Elston Hall Primary School, Fordhouses

Soul Dragon

S uper deadly
O n two legs
U nderground
L ives in mountains

D eadly as a black hole
R oars louder than a lion
A n extreme killer
G argantuan
O n two-metre legs
N othing can kill it.

Christian Betts (9)
Elston Hall Primary School, Fordhouses

My Dragon

M ine, and only mine
Y ou will regret attacking it

D ark, glowing eyes
R oars like a dinosaur
A s strong as a tiger
G liding in the starry night sky.
O nly will attack if annoyed
N ever attack them.

Micheala Kandare (8)
Elston Hall Primary School, Fordhouses

The Unique Unicorn

U nique in its own way
N ever seen a more beautiful beast
I mpressively magical
C andies surround them for celebrations
O bsessed with rainbow hair
R ain is their favourite weather
N ever mess with this unicorn.

Amelia Motsi (8)
Elston Hall Primary School, Fordhouses

Fire-Breathing Dragon

D eadly, fire-breathing.
R are fire-breathing dragon.
A s big as one billion people.
G lowing red eyes.
O n its body, it has glowing scales.
N ever steal the dragon's eggs because it will breathe fire at you.

Jenson Corbett (8)
Elston Hall Primary School, Fordhouses

Water Corn

W atching, waiting
A s angry as the Hulk
T alons screeching
E mbers can be eaten
R eady to pounce.

C urling up is a shiny ash tail
O range face
R ough scales
N ot calm.

Isabelle Martin (8)
Elston Hall Primary School, Fordhouses

Hunting Blaze Hyena

Claws tapping on the ground
Creeping closer
Mouth opening
Teeth ready
Claws ready
Fire swirling round on the inside
Heart pounding
Brain targeting prey
It then strikes,
Slash, *stab*, burn,
The prey slowly dies.

James Hayward (8)
Elston Hall Primary School, Fordhouses

Fire Crab

F ire crabs are dangerous
I t can break icebergs
R elated to a brother
E yes can turn sharp

C an have laser eyes
R eligion is Christianity
A poison crab
B ack is full of spikes.

Alessandro Boneham (8)
Elston Hall Primary School, Fordhouses

My Beast

M ythical unicorn
Y ou wouldn't believe it.

B eing hunted to death
E bony horn shining
A pair of sharp, glowy eyes
S oft fur as white as snow
T wo wings gliding in the sky.

Kate Wilkinson (9)
Elston Hall Primary School, Fordhouses

Cybermen

C ourageous like a lion
Y ellow like a fish
B reathes out oxygen
E yes like an octopus
R aging teeth
M ane is longer than a snake
E agle wings
N egatively annoying.

Presley Keogh (8)
Elston Hall Primary School, Fordhouses

Dragon!

D ark stripy wings
R ideable, you only need a saddle (you need to tame it)
A s big as two schools on top of each other
G reat at flying
O nly 14,569 left
N ear forests, not towns.

Liliana Silba (8)
Elston Hall Primary School, Fordhouses

Lynel

L ion-man beast
Y ou do not want to start a fight with it
N o good to fight
E ven deadlier than Thanos
L ynels rule.

It is furry
Its hair is orange
Its body is brown.

Flynn Ballinger-Heeney (9)
Elston Hall Primary School, Fordhouses

Sunshine Unicorn

Navy, crystal eyes shining as bright as the sun
Emerald horn shining as bright as the sun
Unicorn so fluffy, you can touch it forever
Sun rising brightly like a diamond
Gold lovely sparkles coming out of its horns.

Sara Mohammed (9)
Elston Hall Primary School, Fordhouses

Football

F ootball only curves.
O nly be a fan.
O nly be a beast.
T eamwork.
B e a fan to enter.
A ims for the goal.
L ead to be a captain.
L ead the team.

Ivor Richards (8)
Elston Hall Primary School, Fordhouses

My Dragon

D evious dragon enraged
R aging flesh is smelt
A ppearing hungry, dragon is ready to pounce on its prey
G ushing for sparks
O rgans hunger
N umerous fleshes hanging.

Scarlett Page (8)
Elston Hall Primary School, Fordhouses

The Dark Dragon

D ark as a spider
R oars as loud as a tiger
A s lovely as fun
G reater than an owl
O ver a thousand years old
N ever gets old, it's as old as life.

Amelia Van Falier (9)
Elston Hall Primary School, Fordhouses

Dragon

D ark, glowing eyes
R ed and orange scales
A s tall as Buckingham Palace
G liding across the midnight sky
O pen-minded every day
N ever attack them.

Emma Watkiss (8)
Elston Hall Primary School, Fordhouses

Siko Demon Killer

D ark red and green lizard eyes
R ed, mean, deadly killer
A lways defeats his enemies
G reen glowing skin
O verrated creature
N ever gets defeated.

Caelan Spittle (8)
Elston Hall Primary School, Fordhouses

My Beast

My beast has got talons as sharp as a triangle,
Body as big as a hotel.
Can shoot purple, shocking lightning.
My beast only comes out at night and on Halloween.
Lives in dark, damp caves.

Billy Guest (8)
Elston Hall Primary School, Fordhouses

Clock

C aring of their food and existence
L asts without food for loads of years
O ccurs with darkness
C areless of its species
K eep watch of nocturnal animals.

Owens Osagie (8)
Elston Hall Primary School, Fordhouses

A Creature

There's a creature about,
Watch out.
Look here and there,
Everywhere.
Going in the forest,
My name's Lorest.
I saw a creature
That was... *a teacher!*

Harry Latham (9)
Elston Hall Primary School, Fordhouses

My Dragon Is A Beast!

My dragon is empowered
My dragon is crazy
My dragon is special
My dragon has a loud roar
My dragon is a beast!
My dragon has sharp white teeth
My dragon is a beast!

Olivia Knott (8)
Elston Hall Primary School, Fordhouses

Diamond

D ark glowing eyes
I nnocent, visible
A bandon babies
M agical powers
O bedient animal
N asty talons
D eadly face.

Maseda Bobie (8)
Elston Hall Primary School, Fordhouses

Dragon

D ragon, breathe fire!
R ed eyes like fire
A spiky tail
G reat white teeth
O n the clouds
N ever ever go near one.

Farid Ahmed Ibrahim (9)
Elston Hall Primary School, Fordhouses

The Rare Cobra Syren

Fly, Syren, fly
Higher in the sky
Eat, Syren, eat
Hunt your prey
Sleep, Syren, sleep
And rest for a day
Wake up, wake up
Do it all again.

Peyton Justin (8)
Elston Hall Primary School, Fordhouses

Lion

L ong as the River Nile
I n the wild it's so mild
O ff in the distance, glaring at you
N ot friendly, it's deadly.

Matthew Powis (9)
Elston Hall Primary School, Fordhouses

The Invisible Dragon

The invisible dragon is a rare beast
It breathes invisible water
It's only found by me...
But a very dangerous dragon,
Fear this beast!

Chijioke Nwoye (9)
Elston Hall Primary School, Fordhouses

The Galaxy Dragon

My beast has eyes like the galaxy.
His teeth are like sharp blades.
His nose steaming with smoke.
His star breathing is *venomous*.

Olievia Coyne (9)
Elston Hall Primary School, Fordhouses

The Beast

B lue soft fur
E merald eyes that can shoot lasers out
A nxious beast
S lippy, cold claws
T all horns.

Lilly Sohal (8)
Elston Hall Primary School, Fordhouses

Snakes Of The World

S lithering through the woods
N erve-racking snake
A mazing sharp teeth
K ing cobra
E mpowered snake.

Charlie Jones (8)
Elston Hall Primary School, Fordhouses

The Movement Poem

Fly fast when you have a cast.
Fly slow when you take a bow.
Run, Hydra, run when you are done.
Run, Hydra, run until you are fun.

Hugo Jenkins (9)
Elston Hall Primary School, Fordhouses

Dragon, Dragon

Dragon, dragon, behind the wall
Who is the scariest?
Who's the smallest?
Who's the biggest
Of
Them
All?

Noah Lea (9)
Elston Hall Primary School, Fordhouses

Fly, Dragon, Fly

Fly, dragon, fly

High and high,
Fly, dragon, fly,

To the top of the moon
Be there too
Go on the moon.

Daisy Durnall (9)
Elston Hall Primary School, Fordhouses

Dragon

D ark red wings
R uined face
A ngry personality
G lowing eyes
O ld
N ice fur.

Corey Marsden (9)
Elston Hall Primary School, Fordhouses

My Dragon

My dragon is the coolest
But they're lunatics
They fly high in the sky
As his hot breath
Burns in the cold air.

Bradley Wood (8)
Elston Hall Primary School, Fordhouses

Dragon

D istant
R azor-sharp teeth
A snake
G reen scales
O mnivore
N ever seen.

Reece Archer (8)
Elston Hall Primary School, Fordhouses

Stars

S hiny and bright.
T ingly and light.
A re high up in the sky.
R andom dots around space.
S pace certainly is amazing.

Arthur Jauncey-Wellard (8)
Gladestry Church-In-Wales Primary School, Gladestry

Space

S pace is dark and wonderful
P art of it is scary
A mazing stars
C ertainly amazing
E xcellent moon.

Jerry James (7)
Gladestry Church-In-Wales Primary School, Gladestry

The Mysterious Kitten

Those that wish for
The fur of their dreams,
They must follow
The river of everlasting streams.

Romy Gent (7)
Gladestry Church-In-Wales Primary School, Gladestry

Wintertime

It is wintertime, snow is falling
It is a perfect time to do a Santa drawing
A great time to meet up with friends for dinner
You can also go outside to see the snow glimmer

Do not forget to wear your boot
It is very good for warming your foot
You can run around and play with snow
Even maybe mould it into snow dough

You can also throw snowballs
But beware, it might start a snowball brawl
You might need to go inside and get warm
Your fingers might get quite numb

Winter is one of my favourite seasons
The snow is the main reason.

Iyanuoluwa Oni (11)
St Bartholomew's Primary School, Glasgow

Mother Nature

'Mother Nature's glory
And her simple little story'
My mother used to tell
'Beside the village well
She would lead us to the mountain'
For so many years, I've given
Her healthy branches, clean and shiny
She looks after the creepy crawlies
Waters the plants each day
One of the most caring mothers
With a little story and so much
Glory!

Annie Moffat (11)
St Bartholomew's Primary School, Glasgow

War, War, Go Away

On a dark, rainy night, the ominous thunder is crackling through the trenches.
The constant sounds of bullets pinging off helmets.
Sandbags being punctured from rifles.
The soldier frantically dove into prone,
At the weapons cache containing Lee-Enfield mags,
And the actual rifle.
Also, he got a new helmet,
He sprinted to the sergeant then, stun!
Ears ringing, half blind, stumbling,
Then he collapsed.

Frankie McGuire (11)
St Bartholomew's Primary School, Glasgow

Home

Here I go home to my country,
I think all about the things in Romania,
Beautiful, amazing, loving, lovely grandparents and friends,
The amazing things,
I just like my country,
I can't tell you how much I love my beautiful country,
I miss my country,
So, so, so beautiful views, lakes, places, restaurants and other things,
Here I go home.

Ioana Mandici (11)
St Bartholomew's Primary School, Glasgow

One Cool Capybara

One spooky night,
A random capybara was going for a little walk,
But then he saw water,
Or was it water?

Capybara, see.
Capybara, drink.
Capybara gets pushed.
Capybara, scream.
Capybara, go aah!

Capybara strong!
Capybara cool!

Riley Hart (10)
St Bartholomew's Primary School, Glasgow

Spring

S parkling, spring sunset
P ink poppies popping out
R ats wriggle, wriggling at the beach
I ce cream melting onto the palm of my hand
N ice knotty grass
G reat green eggs.

Kacey McCallion (11)
St Bartholomew's Primary School, Glasgow

Spring

S unny skies are back,
P eople playing outside again,
R eady for the sun,
I ce has melted,
N early summer
G oodbye, winter.

Stephen Ross (11)
St Bartholomew's Primary School, Glasgow

The Macedonian Poem

Macedonia is culture.
Macedonia is family.
Macedonia is Shtip.
Macedonia is places.
Macedonia is wonders.

Macedonia, I miss you!

Deyvid Mitsanov (10)
St Bartholomew's Primary School, Glasgow

The Girl And The Light

It was morning, but it was night a second ago. She asked a woman what happened. She didn't reply. Annoyed, she walked off, following the light. Wanting to go home, she finally turned around and started walking back but she was in a forest. She sat down by a tree.

Suddenly, she saw a nametag. It said her name, Nila. She stood up and ran away. She ran as fast as she could and then she stopped running. She saw a house. She walked in curiously and a bit scared, but it was a really green house.

She saw a younger girl sitting down, staring at a wall, saying nothing because it was a wall.

Maria Lejwoda (9)
St Oswald's RC Primary School, Wrekenton

Space

Space, space, space
How I look at you
With a face
Of wonder and excitement.
I can see the moon, Mercury
Venus, Mars, Jupiter, Saturn,
Uranus and Neptune.
Some astronauts
And spaceships
Are floating next to the mini-stars
Space, space, space
With stars so bright
They give me very
Warm light
To guide me home
To where I play
Now all that there's
To do is look up
At space.

Violet Dixon (9)
St Oswald's RC Primary School, Wrekenton

Nature's Life

Trees are green
Growing wonder branches

Roses are red
For bees to see

Winter is gone
For all the children

Spring is here
Like never before

Hibernating is over
Animals are free

It's summer now
Ice creams pop

So, what are you waiting for?

Go join the fun
Goodbye to lie-ins

The nights are shorter
More playtime, yay!

Elisha Nouaffo (8)
St Oswald's RC Primary School, Wrekenton

Animals

Animals are fuzzy, soft, hard and smooth.
They live in the ocean, jungles, homes, and lots of other places.
Some sleep in the morning, some sleep in the afternoon.
Some animals hide from humans.
Animals have habitats.
Some don't have habitats.
Some live a longer life than different animals.
Some animals have a different body shape when they grow older.
Snakes have different bodies altogether.

Roxy-Judith Murphy (8)
St Oswald's RC Primary School, Wrekenton

The Amazing Nature

Nature is beautiful with flowers and leaves,
But some people may scream if they see bees.
I like to lie down on the grass and look up at the sky,
Maybe after that, I might have some pie.
Sometimes, if I see a ladybird,
I will put it on my hand.
It does tickle a lot,
But it does no harm at all.
But if I see a wasp, I might fall,
Because I will run away.

Ellie-Mae Cooper (8)
St Oswald's RC Primary School, Wrekenton

The Stars In The Night Sky

In the night sky, the stars light up
When I dream, I drool with the galaxy in my head
The moon starts to awake as I sing
And when I sing, I stomp my feet, clap my hands, and sing louder
The moon starts dancing along and waking up the stars
The stars shine brighter than ever and burst out of sleeping.
The stars in the night sky are better than ever.

Anna Galach (8)
St Oswald's RC Primary School, Wrekenton

Outer Space

In outer space, stars are shining bright,
The moon is becoming a different shape and size.
You can see Mars brighter than ever.
Universes, spinning around.

The space is dark,
Go into space to see the stars and all of the planets.
Planets have lots of colours, red, blue, orange, white
are the planets' colours.
The space is quiet.

James Donnelly (9)
St Oswald's RC Primary School, Wrekenton

Environment, Nature

Look after the environment, it can help us very much,
The environment is very good,
It can help us in all sorts of ways,
It's home to ninety per cent of our oxygen,
So, look after the environment and nature
It will help you out a ton,
And when the seasons change, so does the environment,
So, please look after it too.

Isaac Hand (8)
St Oswald's RC Primary School, Wrekenton

Up In Space

Look at the stars, shining bright,
Feel the warm glow of the sun.
The beautiful colours of the galaxy
Will amaze you.
The moon is light and so cool.
Space is an important part of life.
So, when you feel down,
Look up into the universe
And you will definitely cheer up!

Ella Fairless (9)
St Oswald's RC Primary School, Wrekenton

Space

Space is full of interesting things.
Planets, stars and a lot more.
In space, it is very quiet but not empty.
Some things we don't know exist, but some we do.
Some things are scary, but we are safe.
There are things like black holes!
They are very dangerous, so watch out!

Max Nalepka (8)
St Oswald's RC Primary School, Wrekenton

Nature

Raindrops falling, leaves growing, birds chirping.
The trees blowing and you can smell the nature.
Oxygen in your nose, you can hear the deer galloping across the green nature forest.
Mushrooms growing, flowers blooming with colourful colours.
What a wonderful sight of the nature.

Julia Jablonska (9)
St Oswald's RC Primary School, Wrekenton

Mighty Team Space

My poem is about space
There was a magical planet that had opened
It went into a different universe
Through the universe, there is a universe with
Laser guns that can blast aliens
And upgrade your laser gun
Find the portal
Go back to space.

Bobby Buxton (8)
St Oswald's RC Primary School, Wrekenton

The Space Facts

The sun reflects off the moon.
The sun gets hotter and brighter.
Look at the stars across the sky.
Feel the warmness of the sun and glow.
From it now we are talking about it.
Mars is red, it is bright, you cannot see it because of how far we are.

Thomas Reveley
St Oswald's RC Primary School, Wrekenton

The Four Seasons

Snowmen are here
They're happy always, it's winter now
Get your hats and gloves on
And run outside
Don't forget your coat
Then you'll be fine
It's nearly spring
Snowmen are melting
The nights are shorter.

Tommy Alberts (8)
St Oswald's RC Primary School, Wrekenton

Space

The stars were as bright as a light.
Space is as dark as a winter's night.
Saturn, the moon and Neptune,
All planets in space.
Space is beautiful.
The Milky Way is bright.
Look through the telescope,
What a wonderful night.

Jacob Hewitson (8)
St Oswald's RC Primary School, Wrekenton

My Hero

A hero came up to the window.
It was my hero, my brother.
He was tall and smart and kind and helpful.
Everyone saw him,
Everyone was impressed by his skills.
He was a great brother.

My hero is my brother.

Kuba Malocha (8)
St Oswald's RC Primary School, Wrekenton

Newcastle, Let's Go!

Newcastle is a really good team.
When I dream,
It's a really good stream.
I dream about Newcastle winning the Premier League.
When they achieve,
They would play against the Manchester City team.

Scarlett Coulson (8)
St Oswald's RC Primary School, Wrekenton

The Future

T his is what will happen in the future
H ouses will be floating gracefully, and cars will be parked in the air
E lephants will have two heads, one for spare

F un things will be really boring, like going on holiday
U nder all the makeup, there will be ugly faces
T oilets will be useless, so you have to poop on the ground like animals
U p in the sky, cars will be able to fly
R oofs will be invisible and will make you happy
E verything I just said you will see someday, from the two-headed elephants to the hay bales without hay.

Fia Tennant (11)
St Stephen's RC Primary School, Blairgowrie

The Cursed Planet

Have you ever wondered what's outside of this universe?
Well, you see, if you were to go there, you would get a terrible curse.
Most people believe there is nothing there,
But listen to me carefully - this information is not to share,
This strange planet or land is not easy to get to,
But I'll show you how I got there and then you'll believe it's true.
The rocket lands with loud *booms!*
And you then look out to see a colossal building with thousands of rooms,
This building is like ten thousand buses stacked to reach the height of this thing.
The weird thing is, you can magically wish for anything!
Do you remember about the curse?
If you wished for one million pounds, you'd get one hundred million pennies in a purse,
When you look up, UFOs are flying about.
They go as fast as a cheetah, no doubt.
Once, I made a terrible mistake,
I wished for millions of friends, but they were all fake,
I had thought these were the friends that were meant to be found,

Whatever I did, they clapped and cheered,
They still adored me even if I did anything remotely weird,
Their laughs were like hyenas, making you feel amazing,
But all at once, my mini phone goes *ping!*
I looked up abruptly, but they were all gone
My friend was only giving me a ring,
The salty, wet tears dribbled down my face but immediately turned to ash,
So, I left that dreadful planet with only a small food stash.

Amanda Miller (11)
St Stephen's RC Primary School, Blairgowrie

The Curious Mermaid

There once was a mermaid
Who lived with the coral and shiny blue fish
But this mermaid wasn't happy
She only had one wish
Her wish was to explore the black sea
The legends of a dark wasteland
Who wouldn't want to see it?
She grew bored of her colourful rainbow land
So one day, she slipped away
And she swam and swam
And looped and looped around her favourite rock
She got to the gate her father had made and gave it a firm push
But oh this place was cold and sad
She wondered if what she did was really that bad
She swished her fins backwards and forwards, turning left and right
And in the dark, she saw a beaming light
Shuffling forward, her heart pounded and she rushed out
The light moved quicker and with a gentle glow
A sea monster showed his teeth and didn't say hello

She was chased for hours and looped her loop and
swam home
And next time she wouldn't go alone.

Elsie Watt (11)
St Stephen's RC Primary School, Blairgowrie

Minecraft

Minecraft is a game.
Minecraft is fun.
Minecraft is multiplayer.
I play in creative.
I love Minecraft.
I hate Minecraft villagers.
Nice Minecraft is nice.
Nice Minecraft cats are nice.
Nice a raft.
Explosive creepers.
Explosive TNT traps.
Explosive rage.
Craft some tools.
Craft some armour.
Craft a raft.
Right, I need a horse.
Right, run right.
Right, the base is to your right.
Armour, we need armour.
Armour, we don't need armour.
Armour, I need better armour.
Fun, Minecraft is fun.
Fun servers are fun.

Fun, building is fun.
The mobs are cool.
The base is great.
The terrain is flat.

Richard Mcgregor (12)
St Stephen's RC Primary School, Blairgowrie

Bojan Miovski

B anging goals in the back of the net, like Ronaldo
O n the run, teammates playing it through to him, like Kevin De Bruyne
J oining the club, quickly becoming a legend
A lways on the run
N ever missing

M any good goals
I f you're looking for a striker, number nine is the answer: Bojan Miovski!
O n different levels
V ery good footballer
S killed player
K icking it into top bins!
I n the box - he is scoring!

Liam Nelson (11)
St Stephen's RC Primary School, Blairgowrie

Trick Or Treating

Children all around,
Every year all colours,
Sugar rushes all the way.

Karolina Peplinska (11)
St Stephen's RC Primary School, Blairgowrie

Great Dragons

Oh, great dragons of elements and wisdom,
Won't you dare share your secrets?
We crave to know, if only you'd share some.

Gorgeously azure blue,
Oh, water dragon, won't you share your waves?
If only I knew how to persuade.

Full of fury, oh, fire dragon with your crimson scales,
Go on! Share your arduous tales.
Do not fear as you lash your fiery tail,
For I am only frail.

Oh, great dragons of elements and wisdom,
Won't you dare share your secrets?
We crave to know, if only you'd share some.

Spiral through the sky,
Oh, air dragon, please share your secrets
If you could try.

Sprouting with vibrant flowers,
Oh, nature dragon, spread your adventurous vines!
All that time you spent venturing for hours,
We must know all the tales of time!

Oh, great dragons of elements and wisdom,
Won't you dare share your secrets?
We crave to know, if only you'd share some.

Farewell for now, as I search for myself,
I am a strong warrior, so I will not ask for help.
These adventures may be hard and when deciding I may choose wrong.
I will stand my ground and stay strong.
Farewell.

Ava Allen-Goring (11)
Swallow Dell Primary School, Welwyn Garden City

Beware Of The Sharks Beneath The Surface!

In the depths below, where sunlight fades
Lies a predator with power and grace.
Its skin is rough, its eyes aglow
The shark is feared by all below.

With razor-sharp teeth and strength untold
It hunts its prey with a precision bold.
A symbol of power in an ocean wide
Its presence unknown, with a fearsome pride.

But there's more to this hunter than meets the eye
It's more than just a creature below the tide.
It's a creature of mystery, with a history grand
Living for millions of years in its ocean land.

So let us respect the king of the sea
A beautiful creature that's wild and free.
Though it may seem like a thing to fear
It's just trying to survive in its ocean sphere.

Freya Bartell (11)
Swallow Dell Primary School, Welwyn Garden City

Mother Nature's Magic

I wake up, the leaves crunching against my feet. It's autumn time, so my fur is growing thicker. No one else is out yet except for the birds, chirping and tweeting. Oh, oh no, I can see mankind in our forest. I need to warn the others. One of the men is wearing a fur coat and has a rifle on the back of his neck. Following behind is a camouflaged jeep, loaded with men and weapons.
I run to my wolves' lair, whilst howling for others to come. Someone is behind me, holding a dagger. Mother Nature, please help me. I run to my hideout. Jack, Jason, Rory and Jessica are staring at me. They pounce on the man, scratching the front of his dagger. The man sprints away, crying for backup. Mankind has left.
You see, Mother Nature owns the forests. Mankind must leave.

Jack Horton (10)
Swallow Dell Primary School, Welwyn Garden City

The Dastardly Destination

The ice rink-like path,
Stood in front of Harker.

Hastily ascending it,
He saw out the corner of his eye,
His beloved boat,
Was getting battered,
By the tempestuous sea.

Above him,
Caliginous clouds loomed,
Over the weak, fading sun.

Wrapping his cashmere scarf,
More tightly around his neck,
He pushed onwards,
With no further delay.

His beribboned top hat,
Was trying to be stolen,
By the weeping, wailing wind.

As he approached a sinister-looking gate,
He saw above it,
Two grotesque gargoyles,
While the rusting iron gates,

Watched his every move,
As they closed behind him.

Ellis Winward (11)
Swallow Dell Primary School, Welwyn Garden City

We Are All Unique

We're all unique in all types of ways
Don't be embarrassed, you're perfect the way you are
Big, small
Brown, black, white
Legs, no legs
Arms, no arms
Deaf, not deaf
Blind, not blind
Never be ashamed of yourself
You're strong and mighty, nothing can stop you
Just remember one thing for me
Always be positive, kind and safe
Then you will succeed in life as a good person
Be you,
Fabulous you!

Adam Benbassou (11)
Swallow Dell Primary School, Welwyn Garden City

I Write About My Home

My home,
A place to be,
My home,
With my family,
My home,
With all my friends,
My home,
The fun never ends,
My home,
A safe space,
My home,
A wonderful place,
My home,
When I am lonely,
My home,
The one and only,
This is my home,
Others may be different,
The way I have grown,
The home I will always know,
That's why I will write about my home.

Jessica Phillips (10)
Swallow Dell Primary School, Welwyn Garden City

Summer

The sun is shining,
People are smiling,
Blossom trees,
Blooming leaves.

Animals play in the sun,
Never stopping, having fun,
Children playing all together,
Spraying water at each other.
That's why everyone loves summer.

Amira Benbassou (9)
Swallow Dell Primary School, Welwyn Garden City

Aya Powergirl X: The Poem

A normal teenage girl from the suburbs,
Y ou may or may not know her,
A ya Marker loved making manga books,

P laces, characters, all of it anime,
O h, but she then had that one fateful dinner night
W hen a mysterious green portal opened,
E verything counts, now she's a magical girl warrior,
R eady to save the people of Sekai Maho
G irls and boys, she and Cinnamon are here,
I n and out, prepared to fight the possessed citizens of this world,
R ight and left, when will Kage come to stop them?
L et me tell you the answer, it's now!

X is the sign that unleashes her ultimate power!

Sasha Morton (14)
The Belsteads School, Little Waltham

Thrive Class!

T he school is amazing
H umanity is changing
R ubbers are erasing
I magination is growing
V ictory is awaiting
E verybody loves this school.

C asting and performing
L oving and flourishing
A lways looking forward
S chool is the best
S omeone said their class is a mess.

Skyla Kay-Parsons (12)
The Belsteads School, Little Waltham

Countdown Is On

Countdown is Channel Four's world-famous
Letters and numbers show. Two comfortable
Contestants challenge themselves by finding
Words and reaching the target. The clock
That ticks like a metronome of suspension
Counts them down and goes *boom!* at the end.
The team is as terrific as superstars and the
Studio is as bright as the beach.

Adam Morris (15)
The Belsteads School, Little Waltham

Animals

A nimals can be furry and cuddly.
N ot all animals are furry and cuddly.
I nsects move slowly or fast.
M ice are tiny, cute, and adorable.
A tiger's roar is louder than a siren.
L ittle baby turtles glide through the blue lagoon.
S hiny as a fish leaping out of the ocean.

Frankie Witham (13)
The Belsteads School, Little Waltham

On The Bench

You sit on the bench, looking into the view,
A swirl of light glistening at you and butterflies flying in the view,
They land on you too,
But then you wake up, realising it was a dream,
You look outside into the burning wood,
And all is not what it should seem,
As you sigh and fall back to where you stood.

Anne-Marie Smith (13)
The Belsteads School, Little Waltham

Tornado

T wisting dangerously everywhere
O ver the buildings, crushing them all
R ound and around it goes, beware, beware
N ever go outside
A siren rings when it comes
D estroys! Destructive! Death!
O verview of the debris, there's hope for tomorrow.

Angus Macmillan
The Belsteads School, Little Waltham

Cockapoo

C ute and fluffy dogs
O verexcited puppies
C onfused and scared
K icking their tiny legs
A mazing animals
P layful puppies
O n the soft sofa
O utside, playing fun ball games.

Bella Oates
The Belsteads School, Little Waltham

A Mirror's Reflection

I stand before the glass so clear,
A mirror's gaze, so cold, so sincere.
It shows the face, the eyes, the line,
But hides the soul that's mine, divine and fine.
The reflection looks back with a knowing stare,
As if it holds secrets I wouldn't dare.
It whispers of times that I've let slip,
Of dreams I've forgotten, on a fading trip.
It shows my smile, my darkened eyes,
The moments I laugh. The moments I cry.
But deep inside, it does not see
The hidden places that lie within me.
I reach for the glass, my fingers near,
But the mirror reflects what I fear.
For in its depths, it tells no lies –
Just the truth of what the world denies.
Yet still, I wonder what I could say,
If it could speak, or turn away?
For the reflection, though clear and bright
May not truly capture what's out of sight.

Byron-William Booth (11)
Thornhill Primary School, Shildon

Canary In A Coal Mine

Canary in a coal mine,
Too small to be seen,
Too little to be noticed,
Until its song's stopped.

Away in the coal mine,
Where the canaries long to be free,
The gases get the best of them,
They will never be free!

Canary in a coal mine,
Too small to be seen,
Too little to be noticed,
Until its song's stopped.

The calls of terror for such a small bird,
Gases are their worst enemy,
So are the mines,
So that's what makes history.
The history of the mines.

Nell Egglestone (10)
Thornhill Primary School, Shildon

Worst World War I

In 1914, a siren goes,
Everyone was panicked,
It was World War I,
Most of the children were evacuated.

It went on and on for years,
It was dark and full of bombs and blood,
In 1918, it all stopped,
Millions of people died.

Everyone was heartbroken,
But they could do nothing,
After all this, they thought it was the end,
But another war was coming soon.

Gayuni Balasuriya (10)
Ysgol Parcyrhun, Ammanford

Friendship

Friendship, friendship, it never leaves your side.
Friendship, friendship is always there for you when you need it.
Friendship, friendship, BFFs.
Friendship, friendship, together forever.
Friendship, friendship, always there to pick you up when you're feeling down.
Friendship, friendship, I love you too.

Efa Jones (8)
Ysgol Parcyrhun, Ammanford

School

As exciting as a roller coaster
Always teaching us something new
As wise as an owl
My teachers are always planning new lessons to help us learn
As playful as a bunny
My friends are always happy during PE
I can't wait to go to school every day.

Elinor Davies (7)
Ysgol Parcyrhun, Ammanford

YOUNG WRITERS INFORMATION

We hope you have enjoyed reading this book – and that you will continue to in the coming years.

If you're the parent or family member of an enthusiastic poet or story writer, do visit our website www.youngwriters.co.uk/subscribe and sign up to receive news, competitions, writing challenges and tips, activities and much, much more! There's lots to keep budding writers motivated!

If you would like to order further copies of this book, or any of our other titles, then please give us a call or order via your online account.

Young Writers
Remus House
Coltsfoot Drive
Peterborough
PE2 9BF
(01733) 890066
info@youngwriters.co.uk

Join in the conversation!
Tips, news, giveaways and much more!

YoungWritersUK YoungWritersCW
youngwriterscw youngwriterscw

Scan Me!